# Word Art

Nancy Davy

While every precaution has been taken in the preparation of this book, the publisher assumes no responsibility for errors or omissions, or for damages resulting from the use of the information contained herein.

WORD ART

**First edition. February 15, 2024.**



ISBN: 979-8224961016

Written by Nancy Davy.

# Table of Contents

Cover Photo Attribution:

Untitled, by Unknown Author

Source: Bing Image Search, Creative Commons only

Licensed under CC-BY

Challenge Two: Dog Photo, Challenge Three: Dog photo, and Challenge Four: Sweatshirt; from my personal collection

Challenge Five: Golf Ball

Bing Image Search, Creative Commons only– Golf Ball by Unknown Author is licensed under CC BY-SA[1]-

Challenge Seven: Old Barn

Source: Bing Image Search, Creative Commons only

www.publicdomainpictures.net/pictures.net/pictures/230000/velka/old barn-149999693656uxA.jpg

Challenge Eight: Old Shoes

Source: Bing Image Search, Creative Commons only

www.publicdomainpictures.net/en/ view-image.php?image=175609&&&picture=old-shoes

Challenge Nine: Beach

Source: Bing Image Search, Creative Commons only

This Photo[2] by Unknown Author is licensed under CC BY[3]

---

1. https://creativecommons.org/licenses/by-sa/3.0/

2. https://photoeverywhere.co.uk/east/fiji/slides/beautiful_beach.htm

3. https://creativecommons.org/licenses/by/3.0/

Free Stock Photo https: //photoeverywhere.co.uk/east/fiji/beautiful_beach.jpg

Challenge Ten: small Christmas tree

Source: Bing Image Search, Creative Commons only

www.publicdomainpictures.net/
view-image.php?image=170828&&picture=small-christmas-tree

Challenge Twelve: Butterfly in Hand Photo by Unknown Author is licensed under CC BY-SA[4]

Source: Bing Image Search, Creative Commons only

Challenge Fourteen: (1) Tie-dyed shirt

Source: Bing Image Search, Creative Commons only

www.publicdomainpictures.net/pictures/110000/velka/

tie-dye-background.jpg

Challenge Fourteen: (2) Sad Man

Source: Bing Image Search, Creative Commons only

saadman.png (2195×2400) (openclipart.org)

Challenge Fifteen: Grandmother

Source: Bing Image Search, Creative Commons only

Free picture: grandmother, monochrome, people, portrait, handsome, person, face, street (pixnio.com)[5]

Challenge Sixteen: Steam Locomotive Vintage Train

---

4. https://creativecommons.org/licenses/by-sa/3.0/

5. https://pixnio.com/people/female-women/grandmother-monochrome-people-portrait-handsome-person-face-street

Source: Bing Image Search, Creative Commons only

steam-locomotive-vintage-train.jpg (581×615) (publicdomainpictures.net)[6]

Challenge Seventeen: Freewriting illustration

Source: https://courses.lumenlearning.com/suny-esc-wm-englishcomposition1/chapter/freewriting/)

© Empire State College

Challenge Nineteen: (1) Dying Flower

Source: Bing Image Search, Creative Commons only

www.publicdomainpictures.net/
view-image.php?image=25414&&picture=dying-flower

(2) Hearts Linked Free Stock Photo

Source: Bing Image Search, Creative Commons only

https://as2.ftcdn.net/jpg/03/16/54/35/220_F_316543553_

sGxmb976SL58MCRRvOJ05TKR3V3Rqo2Y.jpg

Challenge Twenty: Rocking Chair

Source: Bing Image Search, Creative Commons only

Free images https://c.pxhere.com/photos/0a/6a/
rocking_chair_rocker_old_ramshackle[7]

_mystery_old_chair_abandoned-643949.jpg!d

6. https://www.publicdomainpictures.net/pictures/270000/nahled/steam-locomotive-vintage-train.jpg

7. https://c.pxhere.com/photos/0a/6a/rocking_chair_rocker_old_ramshackle_

## Word Art by Nancy Davy

......................................As a painter speaks in brush strokes

........................................Allow your words to flow

........................................As colors to a canvas

........................................As bright as a rainbow


........................................As a sculptor builds a work of art

........................................And vision guides his hand

........................................Your words can illustrate your dreams

........................................As his stone, wood, or sand

........................................And as music carries us away

........................................On waves of joy or sorrow

........................................Your words can lift and carry you

........................................Through any sad tomorrow


........................................Art can be found in many forms

........................................It can be seen or heard

........................................But there's beauty and there's comfort

........................................ Within the written word.

# Introduction

I'd like to welcome all of you; our returning writers, as well as those of you who may be discovering my writer's challenges for the first time.

My first book, <u>Dreaming in Color</u>, begins with a look at free style writing and gradually turns towards structured writing and poetic expression. You'll find it to be a series of challenges, posed with the hope of honing our descriptive writing skills; and perhaps even prompting the courage to aspiring writers to put a pen to paper.

<u>Word Art</u> now adds another level to our undertaking. We explore journal-type compositions and attempt a free-writing challenge. We examine our life journeys and write about positivity, personal achievements, gratitude and a variety of emotions. We learn about the importance of releasing our grief, and, equally important, celebrating the goodness that life has to offer. We re-visit important literary devices such as repetition, symbolism, and personification as well as some favorite exercises from the first collection and add some extreme (and delightful) syllable challenges.

Each of these twenty challenges is intended to reach into our mind and our heart and draw out something different. I have provided each challenge with an example. These exercises may be humorous or serious; some providing lookbacks on our past or comments on the present.

My intention with both of these books is to illustrate the power of words, and help you discover that the power lies within each of us. Our words can convey a broad range of emotions. They are reactions to our life's blessings and its challenges. They can find humor when sorely needed, share passion, and express grief. All are inspiring. All are healing.

I hope you'll enjoy both of these works and that they may move you; if you have not been already, to also seek a path toward sharing your thoughts and expressing yourself through the written word.

# Dedication

Once again, I'd like to dedicate this book to the members of my Creative Writers Workshop, past and present, that now spans five years. Their courage and willingness to try something new is appreciated more than I can say. I also commend them for their hard work and patience with my efforts. I've been continually amazed at the broad range of responses shared at our gatherings, prompted by our varied pasts and the willingness to simply open our hearts and write.

# Challenge One: The Power of Positivity

As some of you may be trying this for the first time, I'm starting with some beginning exercises that will allow you to 'loosen up' mentally and just write, without requirements as far as structure and form.

We'll begin with a topic that we can all relate to, because it has affected all of us. Let's go back in our memory to the pandemic of 2020 & how you were touched by it. List some negatives. Then list the positives as you see them, and draw them out. If you would like to single out one positive and write about that, go for it.

The idea is to view the negatives, and discover how we all have the power within ourselves to find something positive. Remember that the ability to express and share our thoughts and emotions on paper is always a positive. It can be reparative, and it can be healing – not only to us, but to those who read the words we've written.

Positivity

Positivity is the act of searching for the positive.

Positivity encourages viewing life situations as opportunities, or surmountable challenges. It allows us to draw on other successful episodes in our lives, and enhances our perceived probability of doing well in the present.

Group positivity can create a trusted space, and an empathetic atmosphere from listening deeply. It can relieve stress so one can feel supported.

Examples of positivity: Gratitude, Savoring (past, present, future)

Viewing the Pandemic:

Negative effects:

Stress, anxiety, depression, fear, uncertainty, loss

Positive effects:

??????????????

To illustrate:

### Seeing 2020 by N. Davy

It certainly would not be original to say that this year was unprecedented. We were all caught up in a swirl of shock, fear, and uncertainty. News too terrible to take in more than small doses. Anxiety about the safety and well-being of our loved ones. For many, grief and loss of family members or friends. The feeling of being powerless.

That feeling of having no control likely grew for many of us as we were forced to become housebound, when businesses were closed and we were encouraged to stay home. I can remember that, perhaps more than at any other time in my life, I likened my existence to that of a grain of sand – one infinitesimal speck in the global sea of humanity. There was a sense of weirdness - a struggle to cope; to try to deal with the unknown; to wrestle with this feeling of not being in charge.

Hopefully, many of you who shared these feelings also reached a point in your ponderings when you realized that we do, indeed, have control over how we respond. Life's challenges may sometimes seem overpowering. But we all have blessings that we can savor and appreciate. Family. Loved ones. The unconditional love of a pet. The simple beauty of a Florida sky, or a beach, or a rainbow. We do, indeed, have so much to be grateful for.

Some of us have used our down time to make positive personal strides. We have taken on an exercise regimen, or become avid readers or risen to the expert level in Sudoku or jigsaw puzzle assembly. Some (although I'm certainly not one of them) have even honed our golf skills! But how fortunate we have been, to live in 'the bubble' at our small "age-qualified" community, where we have been sheltered to a large degree from the comings and goings of large numbers of people, and protected from many of the dangers of the outside world. Where we can golf and still be socially distant. Where we can take a 'beverage' or two and go for a golf cart ride with our significant other, to take in the fresh air and the beauty of our little world.

Someday, we'll get back to life as we used to know it. But before that happens, while we have the time, let's go through our photo albums and re-live some moments. Get the recipe file and make an old family favorite. Stay connected by picking up the phone and calling an old friend, and Face-time with the grandchildren. Savor all the times we've had, and look for the good in what we have now. Let's examine our lives and count our blessings. You may be surprised at how many there are.

# Challenge Two: An Open Letter to a Pet

(a practice in free-style writing and expressing gratitude)

Most, if not all of us, have had at least one pet in our lifetime that we have shared a special bond with. This exercise is about unconditional love, and how we might express our gratitude for the many ways in which a pet's love can take our life, and our outlook on life, to a different level.

**Example:**

## An Open Letter to My Dog: Thank You for Being There

As a friend's dog passed on, I reflected on my own dogs—here's what I want to tell them.

◈ Adapted from an article by Amber Carlton[1], Dogster Magazine, Jul 30th 2014

To my dear dog: I wish you could know -- really know -- how grateful I am for you, how much you have changed me, how I'm a better person because of you. But if I had the opportunity to tell you in words you could understand, where would I start? What would I say?

I'd say ...

*Thank you for laughter.*

Because of you, dear dog, there's not a day that goes by that I don't laugh. Even in the darkest times, the bleakest moments, you have managed to put a smile on my face. Whether chasing a squirrel or dancing at dinner, you find the fun in every little thing and encourage me to do the same.

*Thank you for perspective.*

It's true, my dear dog, that sometimes I take myself too seriously. I think too much about work and spend too much time glued to the computer. But you are a constant reminder about what's truly important. With a gentle paw on my leg, you convince me to walk outside, feel the sun, and maybe stretch out with you on the grass. Enjoy this moment, you seem to say, because this moment is all we have and the only one that ever really matters.

*Thank you for connection.*

---

1. https://www.dogster.com/author/amber-carlton

As an introvert, I find it comforting and comfortable to be alone, to shut myself away, to avoid idle chitchat. But you, my dearest dog, have made that impossible. Walking with you is like walking with a rock star. Strangers want to stop and talk, ask about you, fuss over you. Through you, I have had the chance to meet people, and, more than that, you have shown me that making friends is far easier than I imagined. Apparently, all you have to do is smile and wag.

*Thank you for being such a wise teacher.*

I have been lucky to have some great teachers in my life. But you, my dear dog, are among the best. You have taught me the meaning of faith and trust, patience and hope. Because of you, I set out on a whole new life path, and along the way, learned that I'm capable of more than I ever thought possible.

*Thank you for being there.*

In the last few years, I've had my fair share of ups and downs. Hellos and goodbyes. Life and death. Triumphs, failures, and uncertainties. But what never wavered was you, dear dog. Regardless of what was happening around me, there you were in the center, my furry little touchstone. Giving me something tangible to hold onto. Keeping me grounded, whole and balanced.

*Thank you for just <u>being</u>.*

It seems impossible that by not doing anything, you still manage to do so much. Your happy attitude in the morning –- *this is the best day of my life! --* sets the tone for the rest of my day. Sitting near you in the same room while I work helps me focus. Even the moments you're snoring quietly (or not so quietly) on the couch fill me with peace and make me calmer. Just the fact that you *exist* somehow makes life better.

Dear dog, I always say that you will live forever. That I will never have to give you the gift of everlasting life. I know, of course, that's not true. That no matter how much I wish it or will it, that day will come, and when it does, a piece of my heart will leave with you. But I also know that even then, even at the moment it breaks, my heart will be bigger because you were a part of it. My dear, dear dog.

* Your turn: If you could tell your dog anything, what would you say?

# Challenge Three: A Special Fortune

This challenge requires that I tell you a little story first. As some of you may know, we lost our dog, Mulligan, to cancer the month before the pandemic forced a shutdown in 2020. During his life, we discovered that he loved the almond cookies that Chinese restaurants give as 'fortune cookies' with their take-out meals. Whenever we'd get take-out, we would ask that any sauces that would be given with the meal be substituted with extra fortune cookies, or we would occasionally buy a few extra. They were kept in his treat basket on the kitchen island.

After we lost Mulligan, I discovered one lone fortune cookie that was in a bag within the basket. I could not make myself throw it away. Before we knew it, almost a year had gone by and it was the day that we would have celebrated Mulligan's birthday. I had the strangest feeling that the fortune within that cookie would contain a message that came to us straight from him.

Mulligan had come from a kill shelter, and the people who fostered him told us we had saved his life. Because the word "Mulligan" means "second chance," naming him was an easy decision. He had obviously been beaten. It took time for him to learn to trust, but we could sense that he loved his place within our home. As we grew to love and care for him, we also discovered how very much *we* had needed *him*. It was certainly a case of rescuing each other.

I opened the cookie and pulled the fortune out. To this day, I have it taped on his picture that is on his special shelf, and I marvel at how a message apparently so specific to Mulligan and us found its way inside THAT cookie. The fortune reads "A good home is happiness."

***

Aside from the story of that most important fortune, I used to read and save specific ones that I thought applied to my life, or that I found inspiring as I was approaching retirement age. Here are several that I saved over the years:

Don't wait for others to open the right doors for you.

Dwelling on the negative simply contributes to its power.

A journey must begin with a single step.

Do you want to be a power in the world? Then <u>be yourself</u>.

Believe in yourself and others will, too.

Try to channel excess energies into rejuvenation.

Fear is just excitement in need of an attitude adjustment.

You will soon receive the gift of relaxation.

Keep your eyes on the prize and you will find success.

Dreams are extremely important. You can't do it if you can't imagine it.

The problems of today will be buried by the sands of time.

I'd like you to pick a fortune – either one of these listed, or one that you find yourself (online or in your own cookie). Tell us how you can apply the message in the fortune to your own life. Be specific in illustrating the tie from one to the other, but have fun with it.

# Challenge Four: Taking a note from the Letter Journal

We are going to begin by taking a look-back over our lives, an exercise that many of us likely had ample opportunity to do when our lifestyles were restricted by the Pandemic. Try to quietly review every age; all of the memories – the highs, the lows, and what you most remember for good reasons or bad. Take notes for yourself of what you find most memorable, and what you feel you've learned on your journey. Then, choose one of the following:

*Write a letter to your nineteen-year-old self (or younger, at an age you determine)

*Write a letter to your children

*Write a letter to your future self

You may wish to send a message of important life lessons. You might, however, have a particular event that stands out in your mind that you wish to focus on. How ever you choose to respond, whether with humor or solemnity, let us, the readers, feel what you are feeling and be able to trace those emotions back to where they came from.

Example:

by Nancy Davy

Dear 19-year-old me,

As you approach the summer of your nineteenth year, you will likely have some anxiety mixed with your excitement as your wedding day approaches. What will your future hold in store? Are you ready to take on the challenges of being an adult?

I look back over decades of our life to the moment you are anticipating now. I sense your lack of confidence, your self-assessment of never being good enough. If I could reach back through time to share the knowledge of our life experience, what could I tell you to help guide you along the way?

Don't ever forget who you are. Your identity will evolve, beginning as soon as you get married. You'll become part of a life team as you and your husband move out of the area to follow his career. You will both work hard to establish yourselves and take on the financial obligations of responsible adults- rent, car payments, gas, groceries, utilities, insurance, health care, and the like. You'll transform from child to adult in a heartbeat.

Three and four years later, when your son and daughter are born, there will be a transformation of a different kind, and you'll discover that you are not only an extension of your husband, but a caregiver, teacher, and 'everything' to your children: a source of unconditional love and support as you nurture them and help them grow. You'll give yourself wholly, without hesitation, because with motherhood, your life will take on a new sense of purpose.

You will take them to church, to camp, to swimming lessons, dance classes, scout meetings, music lessons, and all kinds of sports. You'll cheer them on, encourage them to follow their dreams and to be the best they can be.

The years will fly. There will be joy; there will be heartbreak. You will do your best to be a good wife, a good parent, a hard worker, and a good example. You'll stand behind your husband. You'll stand behind your children.

But, please, in the quiet moments when you're alone, try to remember who <u>you</u> are. Your dreams and your hopes for the future are important, too, and though setting them on the shelf was your decision and something you did without hesitation, the day will come when your children and all their friends will leave for college. You will then be faced with an identity crisis as you stare into empty bedrooms and wonder: after all the years of being someone's mom, "Who am I? What's next? Do I still have dreams? Do I still have time to pursue them?"

The answer is *yes*. Take enough time through the years to reflect upon your interests, so that when the day comes that you feel it is *your* turn, you will be ready to summon your courage and shoot for the stars. <u>Believe in yourself</u>.

# Challenge Five: The Personal Essay

This challenge is a general, but important, self-examination essay.

What Is a Personal Essay?

* https://www.masterclass.com/articles/how-to-write-a-personal-essay

A personal essay is a piece of writing that serves to describe an important lesson gathered from a writer's life experiences. The essay often describes a significant event <u>from a first-person perspective</u>, and can be done in various <u>writing styles</u>, like a formal essay or as creative nonfiction. Personal essays usually have a conversational tone that creates a connection with the reader. This type of essay can be inspiring and uplifting, or it can serve as a warning to others to avoid the author's mistakes.

Personal essay topics cover a variety of different subject matters. <u>Any moment in your life that sparked growth or changed you in some way</u> can be written about in a personal essay and enriched by your personal opinion.

How to Structure a Personal Essay

A good personal essay should contain an introductory paragraph, body paragraphs, and a conclusion. The standard length is about five paragraphs, but personal essays can be longer or shorter, as long as they contain all three basic sections.

1. <u>Introduction</u>: The first sentences of your essay should include a hook that captures the reader's attention. Provide a personal statement that you plan on proving in the body of your essay. Avoid common cliches like

opening with a famous quote, and try to form a unique connection with your audience.

2. <u>Body</u>: The body of your essay is the meat of your story that should include your main points and personal evidence supporting the thesis statement of your narrative essay. This is where you, as a writer, share how your personal experiences shaped your point of view, and reflect on the knowledge gleaned.

3. <u>Conclusion</u>: Your conclusion should restate your thesis and contain the moral of your story or a revelation of a deeper truth. Review why this essay matters and sum up the things you want the reader to take away from this particular piece.

6 Tips for Writing a Personal Essay

While everyone's writing process differs, there are a few general guidelines to keep in mind when drafting your essay:

1. <u>Create an essay outline</u>. Drafting a personal essay outline first can help you lay out the main points and tone of the message you are trying to share. Your outline will help you figure out early on if this specific moment is worth writing about. Whichever topic you choose for your essay, it must have had a strong emotional impact on you or have taught you a lesson in some way.

2. <u>Start with your intro</u>. Include your hook, state your thesis, and form an emotional connection with the reader. Set your audience up for what your piece will be about and give them something to look forward to.

3. <u>Fill your body paragraphs</u>. Use sensory details about the sequence of events surrounding your thesis to guide the reader through your personal essay. Build up your personal story here to eventually lead the reader to your main point.

4. <u>Be specific</u>. A descriptive essay about a significant moment in your life is much more engaging than a general overview of something that happened to you. Provide the details necessary about real life characters or any particular feelings experienced.

5. <u>Include a conclusion</u>. Summarize what you learned from your experience and what message you hope to pass on to the reader. It might be a difficult or unsettling revelation, but ending on a generally positive or hopeful note can help it feel more aspirational or uplifting.

6. <u>Proofread your work</u>. Aside from checking spelling and grammar, make sure your intent is clear and your narrative is easy to follow. No

matter how good your writing skills are, it's always helpful to reread your own work and ensure you've solidified your story.

Example:

Lifetime Achievement by Nancy Davy

Sometimes in life things happen that just leave us smiling and shaking our heads in wonder. When we moved to an age-qualified, golf community in Florida several years ago, I was not a golfer! I had always worked two jobs and did not have any time to spend at the golf course, the library, the mall, or anywhere I might have considered a pleasurable break from the grind. But, when we moved here, my workload was reduced to one remote job during the six months of late fall, winter, & early spring. Mid-spring through fall was full time up north working on-site at a winery.

That left me free to join a Sunday golf group after I learned the basics of the game. The format of the average encounter, a "points quota" game, allowed me to compete against myself and be rewarded monetarily if I had a good round.

Fast forward to February of 2013. The group held their annual Ryder Cup tournament over two successive weekends. Because my handicap was so high, I was paired with one of the best golfers in our group (an assigned link I'm sure that she was <u>under</u>whelmed with). My score at the end of the first game was so high that I just wanted the ground to open up and swallow me!

I took three lessons during the week between the first and second match. What I did not know is that, when lessons combine with nerves overload, the voices in your head taunt, assess your every move, and scream at you to swing straight, do this, and don't do that.

The second game day arrived, and the format was match play. For those of you who don't golf, that means that you do not count your strokes for each hole as with stroke play. Strokes of the competitors are compared for each hole, and one point per hole is earned by the player who bests his opponent. A tie results in ½ point apiece and the loss of a hole results in no points for the loser of that hole. I played my customary level of dreadfulness for the first three holes.

The fourth hole was a very short par three. I tried to remain calm as I approached the tee box, set my tee and ball, aligned myself and swung through. We watched as my ball sailed upward and dropped on the green near the pin, then disappeared.

Shock! Our disbelief was quickly dispelled as my partner jumped into her golf cart and drove up to confirm that I had indeed scored a hole in one.

It's hard to describe the swirl of emotions that settled over me. Of course, due to the Match Play scoring protocol, my hole in one had not been that much of a help to the team effort. *BUT!! <u>A HOLE IN ONE</u> !!!* This was a lifetime achievement, one that I now understood to be (at least in my case), based on pure luck, not skill. My husband had not yet had a hole in one! (He did get one two weeks later, and now has five!).

As I said in the beginning, sometimes in life things happen that just leave us smiling and shaking our heads in wonder. I remember grinning as I added one more take-away: *"IT'S OFF THE BUCKET LIST!"*

# Challenge Six: Personification (Method 1)

We're going to re-visit the literary device of <u>personification</u>. This method of observation gives life to inanimate objects. I also want you to be aware that expressing your emotional reaction to your observations, no matter the literary device we are using, can deepen the take-away.

We'll be doing some different observations. The first will begin with a loose, relaxed style of writing. I'd like you to observe an area <u>within your home</u>. Then describe it, trying to give life to inanimate objects, <u>WITHOUT SHOWING YOUR OWN FEELINGS</u> (we'll get to our emotional response to our observations in the next challenge). Please note that for this challenge you should be observing from an <u>ONLOOKER'S</u> perspective, <u>not from the first person</u>.

Here's an example: Please note that this was written when we had two teenagers in the house and a husband who played in a men's softball and bowling league.

## Hall Closet

by Nancy Davy (from my book, Dreaming In Color)

You wait in jumbled order for the door to be sprung open. The light reveals a large array of "good" coats on metal hangers, that stand in disciplined precision along the right wall. Opposite, on wire hooks, hang the "everydays", heaped one upon the other. When I sometimes turn the light on and find one lying in a heap, I fancy that they jostle for position in the darkness.

You are plain – small, narrow room, drawing all of your personality from your contents. You hold baseball caps of every color. They look down silently from nails along the walls. Some are worn and dirty; others prized, immaculate.

There is the sense of stifled action as I glance across the floor. Here baseball bats and softballs; faded ball glove in repose. Heavy winter boots and gloves are transferred front to back as seasons alter. A bowling bag rests against the wall, dangling handle torn by years of use. Soccer cleats, a color guard rifle, pushed to the back and buried. Rollerblades and helmet, elbow pads and shin guards, and a borrowed pair of crutches. In the corner, a red golf bag stands at attention.

Waiting, always waiting, they remain. I know they are inanimate, yet I can almost hear them. The light brings them to life and they are tensed in expectation. They dream in darkness of another opportunity – to be plucked by hands and called upon to run; to kick; to soar – or simply to escape the boundaries of your gloomy netherworld, where you can give them nothing but your walls. To me you are a trusted holder for safe-keeping, but they only wish to leave you, for it's only then they live.

# Challenge Seven: Personification (Method 2)

We're going to take our observations to another level. This time, I'd like you to choose an outdoor area. Again, describe it by trying to give life to inanimate objects _from an onlooker's standpoint_, but this time I'd like you to _show your reaction to your observations_.

Example:

Old Barn

by Nancy Davy (from my book Dreaming in Color)

The barn stands, tall and imposing against the naked fields. It feigns indifference. Faded whitewash struggles to cling to its exterior. The door gapes open, great mouth undefended against the onslaught of bitter icy wind. Snow swirls and eddies, settling upon the dirty floor, broken planks, and rusted cans full of rusted nails. Odd bits of lumber, sorted by size, are stacked against the back wall. A couple vintage license plates, enamel old and crackled. Flower pots, tipped over, spew their dirt upon each other, and the gardening tools lie tumbled in a heap. A soft pair of gardening gloves, carefully hung on a hook, wait for their next summons. But the hands will come no more.

A crack of sunlight through broken windowpane falls on shattered glass and dusty boxes and seems to be absorbed there, not radiating far enough to penetrate the dark and musty corners. A silence so profound that you can almost reach and touch it. The smell of dust and driveway dirt. A can of gasoline. Rafters, dry and brittle, are spattered by the swallows that frequent them to roost. Abandonment in wooden form, this structure stands, a shelter now to barn cats, darting transients that seek its darker depths.

Forgotten but forgiving, in a pose of patient waiting, the tired beams support each other bravely. As the wind howls through the rafters, an ache forms in my heart. It is the chilling sound of loneliness.

# Challenge Eight: Personification (Method #3).

Another form of personification is from the first-person outlook, allowing you to become the subject that you are observing. I'd like you to write a story from the perspective of a pair of your shoes, or an article of your clothing or jewelry. Try to use several senses (sight, sound, smell, touch (ex. textures) in your descriptions.

*As an additional level of challenge, try giving the subject you are describing a human struggle relatable to one of your own.

Example: Old Shoes by Nancy Davy

My laces are torn and tangled; my leather exterior dry and dirty, and rough to the touch. I lie in darkness on the closet floor, forgotten. It wasn't always this way. I sigh wistfully and remember the days of my youth.

When I first came here and was taken out of the box, a man picked me up and slid his feet into me. He tied my laces tight and we were off! We worked hard together for years as he would mount a riding mower and travel for what seemed like miles. Then he'd push a hand mower on the banks near the country road where we lived as well as at the large plant where we worked. I would travel up and down the ladder with him as he painted various buildings or painted the guardrails near the plant entrance.

My "new leather" smell is a distant memory, as my outer surface was often spattered with paint before it was discovered and wiped clean. If one were to sniff me at the end of the day, they would be greeted with a mixed scent of sweat, freshly mowed grass, paint and gasoline.

My soles slowly began to wear. I was with "my co-worker" as he ran the forklift, bulldozer, and other machinery, when he worked inside on the production line and even ran one of the large machines during season. His feet were never idle, and neither was I.

But then something changed. I heard the word, "retire." What does that mean? My friend didn't come to get me anymore, and the house became silent.

It's dark in here. I don't understand. Why doesn't someone come to get me? I can still do things! Just because I'm worn doesn't mean I'm worn *out!* Just because I'm old doesn't mean I can't contribute! I'm still useful. I still have value. Someone, *please. Come open the door!*

# Challenge Nine: Making a Sensory Observation

Often, when we make our observations, they can be rather one-dimensional, because

our words don't convey our sensory experience. This happens when we 'tune in' to our senses and focus upon the incoming data, drawn from what we see, hear, smell and touch.

Try sitting for a moment with your eyes closed. As you concentrate on your subject, try to absorb it through one sense at a time. Focus upon your sense of hearing, your sense of touch, your sense of smell, even your sense of taste, if applicable. Describe what your senses processed. Review your finished piece to see if you can further draw out descriptions that are not specific. For example, instead of "the sound of a bird", you might describe it as "a trill or a warble."

The purpose is to focus our attention on the details our senses relate, and fine-tune our descriptions of those details, instead of generalizing, thereby becoming more and more specific in our descriptions.

This challenge is to make a sensory observation. You have the choice of selecting any subject - indoors or out, but this time, DO <u>NOT</u> give life to inanimate objects – rather; describe what you see in detail, <u>using your senses of sight, smell, and sound</u> and then, again, <u>draw your reactions to your observations</u>.

Example: The Beach

by Nancy Davy (from my book, Dreaming In Color)

A cacophony of sunlit sounds live at the beach. I crest the tufted knoll and am assailed with smell of salt spray. Sandals slip off; toes slip into sun-warmed sand as balmy breezes lift my cares and carry them away. Waves roll in from the horizon under summer's cloudless sky.

Here is life, and it is everywhere, and in all sizes. Children splash as waves rush and retreat. Shells sparkle in the shifting sand. Egrets stalk stiff-legged, poking beaks into the sand, then cock their heads and chortle as they find a tasty morsel. Gulls screech and squabble, undaunted by my presence. A sand crab scurries for cover. Pelicans ride the breeze majestically, then wheel and dive.

Brightly covered canvas chairs march in even rows along the private hotel beachfronts; sun worshippers recline. Tinkling laughter and conversation permeates my outer conscience.

I daydream. I walk slowly, watching as my footprints fill with water, then are whisked away by the next tide's pull. How pleasurable, this exercise of just observing nature. It draws me to a yearning to never leave this undemanding place, so full of life and yet so far removed from it.

Priorities are re-discovered here.

# Challenge Ten: Emotional Observations

We've practiced describing a subject with the use of our senses – in other words, describing with the use of our sight, smell, sense of hearing, our sense of touch, and even our sense of taste, if applicable.

I'd like to present a different type of challenge, and that is to give reign to an emotion and allow it to control your description of a given object. Let's pick one inanimate object, such as a golf cart; a ticking clock; Christmas tree or a microwave, just to make random selections. I'd like you to choose three emotions from the list below, then describe <u>the same subject</u> three ways, to see the difference alternating your emotional perspective can make.

Object (pick 1):

Golf cart Ticking clock Christmas tree Microwave oven

Emotions (pick 3):

Anger Surprise Loneliness Annoyance

Sadness Confusion Jealousy Frustration

Happiness Inspiration Love Despair

Confidence Worry Fear Contentment

Example:

Love- by Nancy Davy

My Christmas tree. Who would have thought that a small, slender box could hold such a treasure? And that we could feel such tender emotions for something so simple!

Only four feet tall, you are easy to snap together. You patiently stand as I open the boxes of ornaments and lovingly select my favorites: some from when our children were young, ceramic ones that my late parents made together, some souvenirs from tropical destinations, some with our favorite sports team logos. As each takes a place on your branches you become so much larger than the limits of your tiny stature, for each ornament added is a reminder of the spirit of the season, of the love of family, of our blessings. You truly are a symbol of love.

Despair (in 2020)-

I can't do it. I just can't this year. As the Christmas season of 2020 approaches, I open the cupboard where my Christmas tree and decorations are stored. There will be no travel this Christmas- a global pandemic has forced a shutdown that will reduce our family interaction to a zoom meeting.

So, ok.... we can accept that. Our family members are in good health and that's a blessing. But here, within our own household, it has been a holiday for three; or, more accurately, a holiday for ONE with two onlookers, for several years. During that time, Santa Dog made an appearance at our tree every Christmas and our dog, Mulligan, would sit Christmas morning as Daddy doled out his gifts, then open each one by himself.

But not this year. Mulligan lost his battle with cancer in February. I look inside the cupboard at the box that holds the Christmas tree and sigh. I'm sorry, Christmas tree. Looking at you this year would just make us sad. Hopefully next year.

Frustration-

I am certain that the period of time from Thanksgiving until about the tenth of December goes faster than any other time of the year. So much to do!! How can one possibly do all the shopping, wrapping, baking, writing out of Christmas cards, mailing of packages, and decorating the house, inside and out, in addition to all of the everyday tasks that we need to accomplish? And have you noticed how absolutely irritating Christmas music can be when it's only late November or very early December and your Christmas chore list is WAY TOO LONG?

It takes forever just to find the outside decorations – some are hanging on hooks on the garage wall, but others are buried in totes that are up on the shelves. Those for inside are also scattered; stored in different places, and the wall at the far end of the living room takes a long time to painstakingly decorate. Another challenge is the shelf in the dining room. And don't forget that all of the items that are removed from those rooms to be replaced by holiday decorations must be packed away. Aaaargh! This is too much work!

Lastly, there it is in the back of the cupboard - the small Christmas tree. Quick, unpack it and snap it together. Now, find the boxes of ornaments and get busy!! Once the tree is full of ornaments, put the empty tree box back in the cupboard and set the two ornament boxes in front of it. Plug the tree in. Oh, no! You should have done that BEFORE you added the ornaments! Whew! Thank goodness the lights work!

Ok, decorating is done for another year, and another job off the worry list until it's time to pack up again.

Time for a cup of holiday cheer.

# Challenge Eleven: A Common Concept (?)

Ask fifty people what their perception of happiness is and you may get fifty different answers. The dictionary defines happiness as "a state of well-being and contentment; joy" (Merriam-Webster). But what transports us to that enviable state? That answer might be affected by many factors, including age, gender, family, life goals, financial achievements, and romantic interests. Not only that, but the elusive state of happiness can shift and change as we travel our life path and are perhaps called upon to deal with struggles along the way.

Go back in your memory to an early part of your life. Try to insert yourself back into the image of younger you, and try to remember what truly made you happy at that age. Slowly scan forward through your life, looking at how your perspective changed and how you see things now.

Define "happiness" as you presently view it and tell how that perception may have altered throughout your lifetime. What have you learned about what happiness really means? How does one achieve true happiness?

Example: Happiness by Nancy Davy

When I was young, happiness was playing outdoors. Shared time with family, and conversation around the dinner table on Sundays. Climbing trees, playing ball, and walking down to the corner grocery store to buy penny candy from the glass display case. Our kitten. Christmas morning; the floor around the tree filled with six kids in bright flannel pjs, all opening stockings and a small number of gifts. We didn't have a lot. But we had what we needed- a roof over our heads, food on the table, and clothes on our backs. And each other. We were lucky, indeed. And we were happy.

Until we weren't. My sister Ellen became ill. She missed a large share of first grade because she was too sick to go to school, and over the next several months her health continued to decline. Eventually she was hospitalized and never recovered. She was seven years old when she passed. My brother Tom was twelve, I was eleven, my sister Linda was eight, my sister Jan was five, and my brother John was two. Tom and I were old enough to understand our parents' devastation, and we all learned the meaning of grief, loss, and helplessness. A lesson not fashioned for young children, or for parents; for that matter. Losing a child goes against the natural order, and Mom and Dad would never be whole again.

We did move forward, and there were other family times- camping, singing (my brother Tom taught himself the guitar and wrote several songs). We used to sing together - Simon and Garfunkel, Beatles, folk music, etc. and happiness took on a musical form. Not long afterwards, our church began to do folk masses, and we sang for those.

When I was sixteen, I met a boy, fell in love, and married three years later. Facing the future as two innocents, we hoped that life would treat us well and that we would rise to the challenges it might present.

There were many ups and downs as the years unfolded. The definition of happiness was an ever-evolving beacon as we fast-forwarded through job promotions, moves, our first house, the birth of two babies, and purchasing a business. There was so much joy in being a parent! And yet, happiness began to be also measured by financial stability, so that we could make ends meet and provide a good life for our son and daughter.

At times it was hard to remember that the simple things are really all we need.

Now we're older. We've retired, and our happiness took on a whole new dimension when our grandchildren were born. These days, it's our children's turn to take on the responsibilities- the jobs, the parenting, the constant schedule race with work, school, sports, homework supervising, music lessons, and everything else that can be crammed into a day's time. We know that in a heartbeat our grandchildren will be off to college, and we've watched them grow with pride and pleasure.

We're slowing down. We're savoring our memories, and we're counting our blessings. We are grateful for every day. For our family and our friends. For our dog. For the roof over our heads, the food on our table, and the clothes on our backs. For each other, and for the love we've shared that helped carry us through all our years together and built many cherished memories. We may not have a lot as far as material things, but we have everything we need, and that's what happiness is.

# Challenge Twelve: Expressing our Deepest Emotions

This challenge is intended to draw upon some of our deepest emotions and help us to express them. We have all lost someone we love.

The purpose of this exercise is to discover a broad range of substance as we observe many conflicting emotions, such as grief, loss, shock, survivor guilt, despair, loneliness, gratitude for our own life and blessings, or fear of death. Most importantly, it is to learn the healing value that putting our pain on paper can provide, to ourselves and to others who may also be experiencing loss and struggling to cope.

In a previous season, we had an exercise in which we visited a cemetery and described our observations and our feelings. A tombstone is a stark backdrop, but there are many other more subtle ones as we transition through the grieving process, and I don't want to confine anyone to expressing only one stage of their journey. The following are several examples, to help illustrate different stages of loss and sorrow.

Please look within yourself and try to write something that demonstrates how grief has impacted you. There are no restrictions as to form – you may respond in any writing style that comes more readily to you. I'd even encourage you to do more than one response, so that you can deal with more than one stage of the emotional process.

Example #1: Despair by Nancy Davy (from my book Tears From My Pen)

It's so lonely here without you

since you have gone away

Thoughts of you pervade my mind

as day creeps into day.

*

But memories are intangible

I can't show you that I care

Or tell you that I love you

now that you're no longer there.

*

I cannot listen to you laugh

See love within your eyes

Give you candy, share your day

Have coffee, socialize

*

I miss you terribly, my friend

and clutch your memory tight

I pull it close around me

in the dark and lonely night.

*

Are you free from bonds of pain?

Will our souls one day meet?

These hopes are all that make

my sad despair admit defeat.

*

I'll wish for strength, then wish you well

and wait here patiently

Farewell, my friend, and Godspeed

Please save a place for me.

*

Example #2: Reminders by Nancy Davy (from my book Tears From My Pen)


A month has passed already since you went away

But I see you here in everything I do

You are in the gentle colors of the sunrise

The soft pastels as day is born anew.

*

Smooth strains of lilting music bring your memory

And carry to my mind your image clear

A photograph, a smile, a book, a teddy bear

So many small reminders of you here.

*

And everywhere around I feel your presence

Though you may be far away, you're by my side

38

As day turns into day, I will remember

The legacy you left fills me with pride.

*

And in the gentle gathering of twilight

As the cloaking sky embraces hills below

And stars beckon, twinkling nightlights in the shadows

I feel your love, and oh, I miss you so.

*

Example #3: The Battle by Nancy Davy (from my book Tears From My Pen)

My life has shifted back into its own routine

Seemingly an ordered, hurried pace

And yet a void exists under the surface

My thoughts dwell in a dark, disturbing place.

*

In unguarded moments flashbacks haunt me

Again, I live through tortured final throes

The monitors are neon, drain lines multiply

A respirator pounds staccato blows.

*

"Death, have you no conscience?" screams the emptiness.

Hers was such a loving, gentle soul

You robbed her, bit by bit, of every dignity

In predatory pursuit of your goal.

*

All manner of atrocities administered

Her body a poor victim of your whim

But cruelty found its match in human spirit

And uncompromising strength that lived within.

*

She's gone – you must perceive yourself the victor

But hers, the final triumph, at such cost

And we, who loved and witnessed the long battle

Remain, the living casualties who lost.

*

Example #4: The Cemetery by Nancy Davy (from my book Tears From My Pen and Dreaming In Color)

Your name on a small marker indicates you're there

Buried underneath a shroud of snow

I cannot feel your presence and stare emptily

And feeling unfulfilled, I turn to go.

*

There is another there you co-exist with

A small life that preceded yours beyond

A weathered cross leans wearily into the breeze

And plastic flowers whisper, "They are gone!"

*

Your small plot is surrounded by strange neighbors

Their cold granite marquees scream out their names

And family members often make their pilgrimage

To pay homage to reminders of their pain.

*

I will not try to frequent this new habitat

Don't look for me as Spring warms earth and skies

Please understand, your monument lives in my heart

And I visit every time I close my eyes.

*

Example #5: Wings by Nancy Davy (from my book Tears From My Pen)

The butterfly has left my hand

The fledgling sparrow flown

And I remain, with rooted feet

Marking time alone

*

If I only could have given you

The opportunity

To stay a little longer

To fly and soar with me

 

But winged ones all must migrate

To gentler, warmer skies

And your time had come to join them

I saw it in your eyes

 

I know you'll find a better place

No pain and suffering there

And loving souls who've waited

Will now keep you in their care

 

So fly away, my dearest friend

I shall not hold you here

But know you'll stay here, in my heart

'Til wings can take me there.

# Challenge Thirteen: Taking a Note from the Gratitude Journal

One of the more popular journal types, the gratitude journal, serves to record the positive factors in our lives that we are grateful for. The purpose is to nudge us to look through our day and note the people, the happenings, the "things", however small, that made our day better or made us smile. Developing a habit of doing so can condition us to not only be more appreciative, but to focus on the positives rather than the negatives.

Now, because we are doing this as a creative writing challenge and not a daily journal entry, I would like to see you draw out your observations with some detail to show us how you feel or how you were affected by what you are grateful for.

Example: Grateful by Nancy Davy

At the end of a long and stressful day, it is good to step back, close my eyes, and re-focus on the simple things. I am so grateful for the beauty of the sunset. For the slight breeze that moves the gentle palm fronds. For the palm tree itself, the image of relaxation that seems to lift my spirits whenever I look at one. For our beautiful Florida blue skies. For the sound of birds outside the window, and the sense of being surrounded by the wonder of nature.

On the human level, I am grateful for my family: my husband, my children, my grandchildren, as well as all our family members. I remember that when the pandemic forced a shutdown on travel, we missed many opportunities to see our son and daughter, our son-in-law, and our grandkids. I think it was a teaching moment across the globe to not take a single moment for granted, and we savored any opportunity to Face-time.

Here at home, my husband and I began the daily ritual of a cart ride with a beverage, so we could be outside in the fresh air, talk with each other, and even visit with friends while "social distancing." This is a simple pleasure that we still make time to do, and I'm grateful for that.

I'm so thankful for the wonderful people we have been blessed to know. We had many close friendships up north before we moved to Florida. We were happy to discover so many caring friends and neighbors here, and are so grateful to be a part of this community.

And I am grateful for my dog; our latest rescue. Adopted in September, nineteen months to the day after we lost his precious predecessor to cancer, this little boy has brought sunshine back into our lives. He is the picture of contentment when he is being petted and is the four-footed image of the purity of love.

# Challenge Fourteen: 'Baby Boomer' Humor

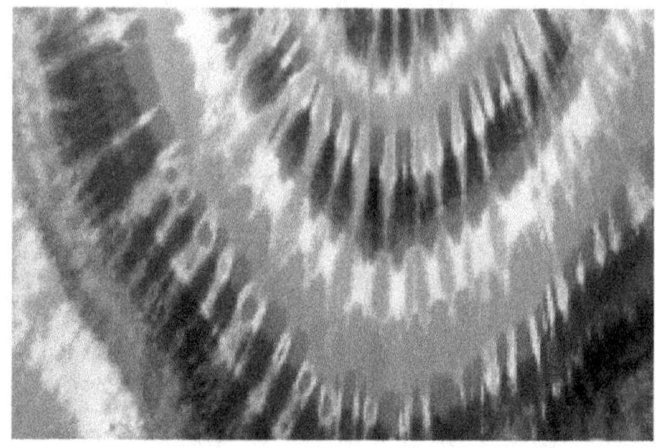

It's time to lighten things up a bit by taking a look at ourselves and poking a little fun – yes, at ourselves, at our lifestyle, and at our aging minds and bodies. A sense of humor is so important, and we need to remember that we can reduce our stress level by not taking ourselves too seriously or dwelling on the negatives. The idea is to compare how we and the world around us have changed since our younger years, playfully jabbing at those differences and trying to find some humor. Here are a couple things to get you in the mood, both appropriate for those in our age group:

- *revised from a social media post, Author unknown

They call us "The Elderly"

We were born in the 40's, 50's and 60's.

We grew up in the 50's, 60's, and 70's.

We studied in the 60's, 70's, and 80's.

We were dating in the 70's, 80's, and 90's.

We got married and discovered the world in the 70's, 80's, and 90's.

We ventured into the 80's and 90's, stabilized in the 2000's, and became wiser in the 2010's.

And we're going firmly through and beyond the 2020's!

Turns out we've lived through EIGHT different decades,

TWO different centuries, and TWO different millenniums.

We've gone from the telephone with an operator for long-distance calls to video calls to anywhere in the world.

We've gone from slides to YouTube, from vinyl records to online music, from handwritten letters to email and WhatsApp.

From live matches on the radio to black and white TV, color TV, then to 3D HD TV with endless streaming opportunities.

Back in the day, we went to the video store and now we watch Netflix.

We got to know the first computers, punch cards, floppy disks and now we have gigabytes and megabytes on our smartphones.

We wore shorts throughout our childhood and then long trousers, Oxfords, flares, shell suits and blue jeans. (And don't forget the tie-dyed shirts with the "Peace" sign on the front!)

We dodged infantile paralysis, meningitis, polio, tuberculosis, swine flu and now Covid-19.

We rode skates, tricycles, bicycles, mopeds, petrol or diesel cars and now we drive hybrids or electric.

Yes, we've been through a lot, but what a great life we've had!

They could describe us as "Exennials" - people who were born in that world of the fifties, who had an analog childhood and a digital adulthood. We've kind of seen it all!

Our generation has literally lived through and witnessed more than <u>any</u> other in <u>every</u> dimension of life.

It is <u>OUR</u> generation that has literally adapted to change.

A big round of applause to all the members of a very special, not to mention <u>UNIQUE</u> generation!

Next, to continue the Baby Boomer theme:

# CONCERNS FOR BABY BOOMERS...Then & Now (condensed)

Then: Long hair Now: Longing for hair.

Then: Keg Now: EKG.

Then: Acid rock Now: Acid reflux.

Then: Moving to California because it's cool.

Now: Moving to California because it's warm.

Then: You're growing pot. Now: You're growing a pot.

Then: Disco. Now: Costco.

Then: Rolling Stones Now: Kidney Stones

Then: "Whatever" Now: Depends

Then: Seeds & stems. Now: Fiber.

Then: Popping pills, smoking joints. Now: Popping joints.

Then: Getting out to a new, hip joint. Now: Getting a new hip joint.

And..., my all-time favorite:

Then: Hoping for a BMW. Now: Hoping for a _BM_!

*Author unknown


Here is a joke that a member of our writing group recalled from memory and shared during our 2021-2022 season (original source unknown):

Two elderly women were out at Perkin's eating lunch. One of them noticed something odd about her friend. She kept looking at her, trying to figure out what was going on. Her friend finally said, "Why are you staring at me? Is something wrong?"

"Well," she replied, "I couldn't help but notice that you have a suppository in your ear. Am I right?"

Her friend replied, "I'm so glad you found it! I wondered where I had put it. Now I know where my hearing aid is!"


Funny Quotes about Aging condensed from Reader's Digest (RD.com,

Arts & Entertainment, Quotes. Sarah Vincent, updated October 17, 2023)

"You don't stop laughing when you grow old, you grow old when you stop laughing." George Bernard Shaw

"By the time you're 80 years old you've learned everything. You only have to remember it." George Burns

"The really frightening thing about middle age is that you know you'll grow out of it." Doris Day

"People ask me what I'd most appreciate getting for my eighty-seventh birthday. I tell them, a paternity suit." George Burns

"At age 20, we worry about what others think of us. At age 40, we don't care what they think of us. At age 60, we discover they haven't been thinking of us at all." Ann Landers

"You are only young once, but you can stay immature indefinitely." Ogden Nash

"Today is the oldest you've ever been, and the youngest you'll ever be again." Eleanor Roosevelt

"Do not grow old, no matter how long you live. Never cease to stand like curious children before the great mystery into which we were born." Albert Einstein

"Aging is an extraordinary process where you become the person you always should have been." David Bowie

"The longer I live, the more beautiful life becomes." Frank Lloyd Wright

"Those who love deeply never grow old; they may die of old age, but they die young." Ben Franklin

"Anyone who keeps the ability to see beauty never grows old." Franz Kafka

"Getting old is like climbing a mountain; you get a little out of breath, but the view is much better!" Ingrid Bergman

"Grow old along with me! The best is yet to be." Robert Browning

"Laughter is timeless. Imagination has no age. And dreams are forever." Walt Disney

"Old age isn't so bad if you consider the alternative." Maurice Chevalier

"Life is like a roll of toilet paper. The closer you get to the end, the faster it goes." Anonymous

"Age is an issue of mind over matter. If you don't mind, it doesn't matter." Mark Twain

"There is a fountain of youth: it is your mind, your talents, the creativity you bring to your life and the lives of people you love. When you learn to tap this source, you will truly have defeated age." Sophia Loren

Next is my example of a humorous poetic look at aging. You may respond to this challenge in any writing style you wish – no restrictions as far as form – just have fun with it.

## Senior Moment

Nancy Davy (from my book, Dreaming in Color)

Morning comes, the day dawns clear

The first day of another year

Resigned; he shuffles to the mirror

And finds confirmation of his fear

The evidence can't be denied

This 'old man' is sixty-five.

.

His gaze sweeps slowly from head to toe

Where did that youthful figure go?

Just yesterday, it seems, his knees

Could take him anywhere with ease.

Now, sadly, he must come to grips

With growing waist and spreading hips

.

The tell-tale signals are all there

The climbing forehead, graying hair

And little lines around the eyes

Offer his age no disguise.

His foggy brain, in youth a 'whiz',

Now can't recall what day it is.

*

Internally, it's much the same

His diet has become quite tame.

Bran and decaf isn't yummy

But gentler on an aging tummy

And little aches and pains abound

It's quite a chore to move around.

*

He spends more time in contemplation

For what purpose his creation?

Were goals accomplished? Did he succeed?

Where will his too-brief future lead?

The sands of time too quickly flow

Where did the carefree youth years go?

*

Evening comes, the night sky clear

The first day of another year

Draws to a close; life races by

Unheeded, save for one small sigh

The world will go on with their lives

But this 'old man' is sixty-five.

# Challenge Fifteen: Shaping a Quote

55

I'm bringing back an exercise from my first book, Dreaming in Color; this time with a different example. I'd like you to go to a public place (indoors or outdoors), and listen to the conversations around you. Jot down expressions or exchanges that are interesting or strike you for some reason. Then write something, selecting a quote from a stranger to begin and end your challenge. Be inventive in creating "the middle" so that it will illustrate a reason that the statement was made.

Example:

Tech Gone Wrong by Nancy Davy

*"Oy, vey! Oy, vey!"* I heard her say.

She waved her arms and walked away.

Fed up with what she termed "a mess",

that described our generation's dress

.

Long hair, tie-dyed shirts, sunglasses,

and torn blue-jeaned long legs and asses.

"Young people, what is *wrong* with you?

and what is our world *coming* to?"

.

I recall that Grandma's point of view

did mellow as her grandkids grew;

took responsibilities upon their shoulders

we all blended in as we grew older.

.

She's gone now, but her words remain

in my memory as a soft refrain

as I look at *this* generation

Who has an endless fascination

For cellphones, gaming, Facebook feeds

that block human interactive needs

family time together, conversation,

replaced now by our separation.


It seems to get worse every day

*It doesn't have to <u>BE</u> this way!!*

Frustrated now, all I can say

Is "Put down the *<u>phone</u>, ok? <u>Oy vey!!</u>*"

# Challenge Sixteen: Symbolism

We're going to take a look at another literary device; symbolism. You'll begin by choosing a word from the list of Symbols, and tie it to a word from the list of Concepts, or create ones of your own. Write a story or a poem in which you associate the object with the concept.

Note: Feel free to add any symbols and concepts you can think of. Also, your response can be in whatever format is most comfortable- free style or poetic.

<u>Symbols:</u>

Crumpled blanket

Torn teddy bear

Kayak

Puppy

Sunshine

<u>Concepts:</u>

Loneliness

Sorrow or loss:

Spirit of Adventure

Innocence

Hope

Example: Lonely (symbol: old train concept: loneliness)

adapted from a poem by my father, R. Edward Ostrander

There's a railroad train down on the tracks

With its metal all rusty and brown

It's the same old train that, at 4:15,

Used to blast its way through our town.

*

Ma would set her clock by its whistle

And I'd thrill to its awful sound

As it made fantasy engineers

Out of every boy around

*

I always felt sorry for that mighty train

Confined as it was to its track

Somehow, I felt that if it were free

That train would never come back

*

Now here it rests on its tarnished rails

And stares with an unseeing eye

And when it's very quiet

I think I can hear it cry.

*

The boxcars are filled with memories

As it sits like a great unshed tear

With the wind as its conductor

And God as its engineer.

*

The other boys are gone now

And I'm sure the tale is told

About the man who talks to the train

As together they grow old.

# Challenge Seventeen: Freewriting, then edit and polish.

The following is a different form of writing prep and follow-through that allows us to identify our strongest feelings. We're going to explore the exercise of freewriting by doing two sessions of the five-minute writings described below. The two sessions of three can be done the same day (morning, then afternoon) or over two days. You'll end up with six resulting freewrites. The next step will be to take a highlighter and read through each result, highlighting any common threads and thoughts you feel are worth saving. Then, compose one article, drawing your thoughts and observations into one polished work. The subject will be determined by where your freewrite takes you. (** © Empire State College,

https://courses.lumenlearning.com/suny-esc-wm-englishcomposition1/chapter/freewriting/)

## Freewriting

Freewriting helps you identify subjects in which you are interested. It assumes that you know your interests subconsciously but may not be able to identify them consciously, and it assumes that you can bring your interests into consciousness by writing about them (as writing equals thinking). Freewriting is like stream-of-consciousness writing in which you write down whatever happens to be in your thoughts at the moment. After you do a number of freewritings, you may find that you have come back to certain subjects again and again. Repeated subjects are good for further development through writing, as they obviously are important in your thoughts.

To freewrite, use your computer or get paper and pencil, whatever is more comfortable for you. Get a kitchen timer or a watch. Write down whatever comes into your head during five minutes without concerning yourself with complete thoughts, whole sentences, or correct spelling or punctuation. Don't even be concerned about making sense in the writing. Just concentrate on recording your thoughts and filling as much space as possible before the five minutes elapse. If you can't think of anything to write, just write "don't know don't know" until you have other thoughts. If you think that this exercise is stupid, then write "this is stupid this is stupid" until you have other thoughts. Remember, the purpose of freewriting is to fill as much space with as many words as possible in the five minutes of writing time. After the first five minutes, rest a minute and read over what you have written, then follow the procedure at least two more times. Stop at this point and do something else. Do another series of five-minute freewritings later in the day. You may be able to discern common threads (repeated ideas) after you do a number of freewritings. The ideas you repeat are good ones for essays as they obviously are ideas that interest you.

Sample of Freewriting

Read the following set of three freewritings. Can you find recurrent thoughts that would be interesting for the writer to develop?

Freewriting #1

freewriting. don't know. don't know. this is harder than I thought it would be. worried. what if I don't have any ideas to bring out. the writer's perpetual concern–lack of ideas. Cliches. wonder how they got started? had meaning at one time. say "every dog has his day" now and people will jump at you for using sexist language. don't know. don't know. don't know. don't know. hear the timer ticking. time. so much to do and so little time to do it in. what is time? arbitrary or not? different for different people. so many people pressed for time now. wonder if time went more slowly in grandparents' day, if they needed 24 hrs. to do what we now do in 12. they had to use washboards, coal heat. greenhouse effect. are we greenhousing? greenhouse should have a nice, flowering plant connotation, not self-destruction. destruction by plants. Little Shop of Horrors. plants going crazy. at least the weeds in the garden do.

Freewriting #2

don't know. don't know. don't know. don't know. don't know. wish the 5 min. would go faster. fast time. slow time. fast time when you're doing something you like. slow time waiting in dentist's office or in any place where you'd rather not be. Slow time for children waiting for something special to happen and fast when it's happening. hard to write write write write write. right. what is right? Orville and Wilbur were Wright. bad puns to fill the 5 min. Why do people groan at puns? wonder how that got started. don't know. don't know.

Freewriting #3

do not like bugs in summer. flies and mosquitos, the worst. Read somewhere that June is "kill the filthy fly" month. I agree. hate those large flies that buzz you, usually when you're trying to eat lunch. read about cluster flies recently. they seem to cluster around your coffee when you go out of the room. then the big question, did they dip into it or not?

mosquitoes as bad at night. like dive bombers in your ears. don't know. don't know. don't know. there are other annoyances, part of everyday life. call waiting, caller id, especially when you're on the calling end. telephone solicitors. door-to-door salespeople. rude people in general. the person in the express line at the supermarket with 20 items in the cart. could go on about this one.

One obvious topic for this writer seems to be "time," or the different ways in which we perceive time (adult vs. children's perception of time, how time is counted in sporting events, etc.). "Annoyances" may be another topic, as the writer mentions that he/she "could go on about this one." Actually, any topic mentioned here is a possibility for an essay ("bugs," "cliches," "greenhouse effect," "puns"); the choice depends on the writer's purpose (research or non-research writing?), interests (for which topic can I most easily generate information?), audience (what will interest my readers?), and parameters (what is the type of writing assigned?).

Freewriting is most often used to develop a topic, but it can also be used if you have a topic and don't quite know how to approach it. It's a useful writing strategy.

**© Empire State College

My Example, with Final Essay: (Please note that this was written at the end of 2022, after Hurricane Ian)

Freewriting: First set by Nancy Davy

#1 "Alexa- set the timer for five minutes."

Ok. Now what? This is so hard – I can't write like I used to be able to. I don't mean that the thoughts don't come (although that can be more challenging than it used to be)- but my handwriting is messy and sometimes a little shaky. I would *like* to be able to attribute this to something other than age, so am blaming it on the fact that I don't spend time writing by hand like I used to when I was working – or even when I was younger, before advances in technology in recent years...

#2 "Alexa- set the timer for five minutes."

To continue that thread, recent years and the advancement of technology has caused us all to put our pens down and stop writing by hand. Letters are now obsolete. Thank-you cards? Not hand-written. Everything is done by texting or e-mail. No more penmanship taught in school. A lost art, for sure, so I guess it's understandable that my handwriting is so messy. It's like singing – when you do it a lot, your muscles and vocal chords are in shape; stop singing all the time...

#3 "Alexa- set the timer for five minutes."

To continue- if you try to sing well after not having done it for some time – guess what? You sound terrible!! Those muscles are out of shape and it would probably take quite some time before anything I could sing might be appreciated by listeners. Staying in shape by repetition of movement – handwriting; singing. Don't even get me started on the other muscles! This getting older is not for the faint of heart. I need to start working harder.

Freewriting: Second set by Nancy Davy

#4 "Alexa- set the timer for five minutes."

A New Year. Hopefully a better year. So many family members and friends with serious health issues. So many prayers and so much worry.

Then the hurricane. Just thrown in for good measure? Trying to stay positive became the ultimate test. Now, at the end of the stressful year- health issues could not have hit any closer to home. My husband and I both facing medical issues and looming tests. Cancer? Maybe. Hope not. Prayers for strength as we venture by tiptoe into this New Year.

#5 "Alexa- set the timer for five minutes."

Getting older. What does it mean? Retiring. No more structured hours of every day. Free time to do what we want. Slowing down. Not just mentally, pace-wise, but our bodies as well. Memory not functioning on all cylinders sometimes. Why ARE they called the Golden Years? I wish I could go back and pick an age to be again – but without the demands of working two full-time jobs. Dream on, little girl.

#6 "Alexa- set the timer for five minutes."

So, this is the time and the season for looking back, for self-examination. For thinking about what we need to do differently going forward, to not only help ourselves by perhaps eating more healthily. By exercising. By trying harder to stop worrying about the things we can't control. To remember those we love who are facing health issues, and to be sure to reach out to let them know you love them while you still have time.


Challenge #14 Finished Composition by Nancy Davy


It must be a normal chain of progression that the end of one year and the transition into another prompts self-reflection and feelings about aging. We sometimes shift the blame for physical shortcomings to getting older, when, in fact, there has been a slip of discipline or of steady practice on our part.

This time of year causes us to take a hard look to see what we may be doing wrong, and ask ourselves what we can do to make it right. Hence the compulsion to make New Year's Resolutions; as we perceive the unfolding year to be a clean slate.

I've reached an age considered by some to be old. That's a relative term, but I've at least been around long enough to have learned some important lessons, as each year seems to bring witness to more illness and loss of those dear to me.

So...resolutions? Here's one. Be grateful. For every day we're given. For those we love- our family, our friends. Try to remember that we don't have the power to control our lives. The future may or may not include us, so try not to look so far forward.

Live for today. Be kind. Be a good person. Treat others as you would like to be treated, and practice positivity by savoring the blessings of every single day.

# Challenge Eighteen: Syllable Challenge

Write an eight-line composition using the following constraints:

1.First and last lines use only one syllable words.

2. Second and seventh lines use only two syllable words.

3. Third and sixth lines use only three syllable words.

4. The fourth and fifth lines use only four syllable words.

You can count hyphenated words as one word. You can use your phone or computer to look up one, two, three and four syllable words and make a pile of each to draw from, or type in specific words for your search engine to define and provide synonyms in varying lengths. If you use Word on your computer you can type in a word that you are thinking of and click on Review, then Thesaurus to give you synonyms so you can select words with that meaning and with the correct number of syllables. Or, if you are "old school" and don't want to go the computer route, you can get out the dictionary or thesaurus book and go from there. I should warn you that this challenge will drive you crazy. It is like doing a tough jigsaw or word puzzle, and it's hard to put it down or to stop with just one. There is a huge benefit in studying lists of words, so we can hone our descriptive skills by selecting words that most closely convey our meaning. In addition, examining words of varying lengths helps us find the right tempo within our work (especially helpful with poetic expression). Hint: Be very careful to go back and re-count the syllables in every single word of every line- it's easy to accidentally slip in a two-syllable word in a one-syllable line! Choose a topic, then draw from your groups of words to build your composition. Try doing more than one if you can.

<u>Example One</u>: by Nancy Davy

1 How do I tell you how I feel?

2 Blistered, broken inside.

3 Existence overlooked,

4 Undervalued, disrespected, unimportant.

4 Condescension overwhelming,

3 Depression unending

2 Blistered, broken inside.

1 There! That's it! I tried. (Sigh)

<u>Example Two</u>: by Nancy Davy

1 This is dumb and I can't do it!

2 Counting vocal cadence isn't normal!

3 Restricted expression inhibits liberty!

4 Conventional conversation's necessary!

4 Unorthodox calculating's ridiculous!

3 Suggestion: natural bantering,

2 Relaxed, spoken freedom

1 And "just plain talk" is what we need.

<u>Example Three</u>: by Nancy Davy

1 I dreamed that as we slept we all turned green.

2 Racial bias vanished!

3 Imagine!! World-reaching empathy!!

4 Universal equality! Nonexistent hostility!

4 Implausible? Impossible? Ridiculous?

3 Radical idea? Silliness? Negative.

2 Merely wishful thinking......

1 It _would_ be nice if we could all be friends.

<u>Example Four</u>: by Nancy Davy

1 What a fun task you gave us this time!

2 <u>Kidding</u>!! Writing metered verses?

3 Difficult annoyance overload!!

4 Examining grammatical, syntactical compositions,

4 Meticulous undertaking notwithstanding- ...interesting discovery!

3 Limitless expressions, including accurate selections

2 Really exist! <u>Teaching moment!</u> Finding wordage showing exact meaning

1 This trick will help me as I learn to write. <u>Now</u> I get it.

# Challenge Nineteen: Repetition

An important literary device is repetition. Repeating a word or particular line, at various planned points of your composition, can be a powerful tool in driving a point home, can help create a tempo (as with poetic expression), or can be a gentle reminder of what you'd like your readers to take away from your work. This challenge is to practice with the effectiveness of repetition. You can also try using sentence fragments to bring images together, as with the first example.

Example #1:

The Human Spirit by Nancy Davy

This is how to break the human spirit

Listen very carefully and you can learn to do it.

I've seen it done so many times that I've become an expert.

It's an art perfected over time.

It starts out rather slowly. We learn to take for granted:

Stop looking at attractions and begin to notice flaws.

Impatience on occasion. From time to time a quarrel.

The frequency begins to escalate.

It starts out rather slowly. The bud begins to blossom.

It tentatively turns its untouched face into the sun.

This is how you do it. Never say, "I'm sorry."

Don't appreciate kind gestures and learn to hold a grudge.

This is underrated and can't be taught too quickly –

It takes years of concentrated effort.

Do not bolster hopes.

Don't encourage dreams.

Don't take time to talk: above all,

<u>Don't take time to listen.</u>

It starts out rather slowly. The bud begins to blossom.

Full of hope and promise as it opens to the world...

This is how you do it. Choose your words like weapons.

They can be hurled like daggers, but they leave a bigger scar.

A pain that lives forever. Festering within us.

Even as effective – what's intentionally unsaid.

This is how you do it. Withhold all affection.

See how profound the loneliness of living with another?

Never offer comfort. Or support. Or reassurance.

Just disdainful glances or a disrespectful stare.

It starts out rather slowly. A tender stretch towards sunlight.

Then blossoms quickly pinched until they all fall from the stem.

Dreams are dropped like petals.

This is how to break the human spirit.

This is how to cause the greatest pain.

Watch the hope within now as it withers, wilts, and falters.

So unsure, unsteady. So filled with self-doubt.

So fragile, like a flower.

(You say you saw me drop something?

Oh, it was unimportant.)

It all ends rather slowly...

Example #2:

## An Anniversary Reflection

by Nancy Davy (from my book, Tears From My Pen)

"'Till death do us part"

That promise was spoken

One day on the calendar

Now serves as a token

It holds bright tender memories

Of young, wistful faces

Dreams to reach out for

Unconquered places

The sky was the limit

No bars to success

You had such a love

You were so richly blessed.

Next came the children

And then flew the years

A whirlwind of laughter,

Of love, and of tears,

Occasional times

Love was put to the test

When dreams came apart

When workdays were stressed

But through every hardship

A look; a caress,

And the knowledge that you

Had been so richly blessed.

Should you now close the scrapbook

Because one life is over?

No! Savor each picture

From cover to cover

These treasures have made you

Who you are today

And the love that you shared

Has not passed away

"'Till death do us part"

One heart laid to rest;

But this day we will celebrate

Two lives so richly blessed.

# Challenge Twenty: Observing the passing of time

Write about measuring time with something not expressly intended for that purpose, like cracks in a floor, scuffs on a boot, or weeds in the flowerbed. Draw out your observations and tell how you have been touched by the subject you are observing, adding your own memories as the years have passed.

Example: Rocking Chair by Nancy Davy

The attic room is silent as the door scrapes open and light from the hallway penetrates, touching upon stacks of cardboard boxes, plastic totes, and; in a spot of honor; the wooden rocking chair. She smiles fondly as she recalls many hours of rocking their children, singing to them softly, and dreaming of the future they would share. The tall wooden chair, once glistening with new varnish, was a welcome addition to the nursery as they prepared for the arrival of their babies over forty years ago.

The floorboards creak as she makes her way across the room. She reaches to touch the dusty chair lovingly, noting a small cobweb between the upper rails. She wipes it away and sits.

The dry wood sends out a small squeal of protest. She remains seated, leaning forward to reach inside an open box marked "Toys."

A teddy bear, worn and abandoned, meets her hand. She brings it close and is struck with a wave of memories. This little guy was dragged, squeezed, and transported for many miles over the years when their son was a toddler, a preschooler and even a primary school student. That little face, those large, round, searching eyes, that soft fuzzy body gave comfort in ways that sometimes no one else could, in the quiet moments when he was settling down to sleep, when the day had been demanding or he needed a friend. The little bear was cried upon, whispered to, and spilled upon. And he was trusted and loved beyond measure.

She places him on her lap and reaches in again. This time her fingers find a rag doll. She strokes it lovingly and recalls their daughter's face; contented as she snuggled her companion; those red braided pigtails and stitched-on smile bright against the pillow.

Where did the years ago? It seems like only yesterday that she rocked gently, in this chair, with this bear, with this doll, with their babies – singing softly, dreaming and savoring their blessings. Now they're grown and gone. She hugs the worn and faded toys and thanks them for the love they gave so freely.

She sighs as she begins to rock once more. Again, the dusty, creaking floorboards speak out, adding to the evidence of how much time has slipped away.

# Summary


I hope that you've enjoyed this collection of writing challenges, and that you'll take some inspiration from these pages as you move forward with your own writing journey.

We all have moments in our lifetime that we reflect on, for various reasons, and I've learned along the way how very important the act of putting our feelings on paper can be. Whether you decide to share them or keep them to yourself as with a personal journal, please always remember the take-away in my title poem:

Art can be found in many forms

It can be seen or heard

But there's beauty and there's comfort

Within the written word.

Thank you for reading <u>Word Art</u>, and I wish you all the very best.

Sincerely,

Nancy Davy

# About the Author

I grew up in a small town in upstate New York, as part of a large family. I've always had a love of reading and writing, and when I was younger, a dream accomplishment was to one day write a novel. I began one, but my life was so busy that the dream was put on the shelf. About twenty-five years later, after retiring, the book notes were dusted off and HOW FAR WE HAVE COME began to take shape.

Then the pandemic hit. The forced slowdown provided lots of time to focus, and the stories that had been held inside for so long continued to spill out. Soon there were six novels in what came to be known as The Clairemont Series - a contemporary romance collection. The reading order is as follows: HOW FAR WE HAVE COME, FOR EVERYONE, SOMEONE, SECOND CHANCES, MEANT TO BE, WORK IN PROGRESS, and MORNING BOOST.

The series is set in the small town of Clairemont, Connecticut- a fictional town with heartwarming characters whom you'll grow to love as one story leads to another. Through these stories, we learn that life can always hold promise, and that love can be found at any age.

I've since written an additional series of three contemporary romance offerings, known as The Stephens Point Series. The reading order is as follows: <u>THE NEXT LAP</u>, <u>RIGHT PLACE AT THE RIGHT TIME</u>, and <u>NEVER SAY NEVER</u>.. This series also follows characters you'll come to love, and is set in a rural town in far upstate New York.

I'd like to encourage anyone with a love of writing to follow their dreams, no matter how long the journey. The sense of accomplishment at realizing a dream goal is worth the time it may take to get there

*For those of you whose interests go beyond contemporary romance, <u>TEARS FROM MY PEN</u> is a collection of poetry that deals with grief and loss. It was written after losing my mother to pancreatic cancer several years ago.

I currently head an adult Creative Writers Workshop in southwest Florida, where my husband and I now reside. I have also written <u>DREAMING IN COLOR</u>, and <u>WORD ART</u>, two creative writing tools intended to hone descriptive skills and prompt deeper and more meaningful expression.

# Don't miss out!

Visit the website below and you can sign up to receive emails whenever Nancy Davy publishes a new book. There's no charge and no obligation.

https://books2read.com/r/B-A-AXFK-BKJVC

**BOOKS 2 READ**

Connecting independent readers to independent writers.

# Also by Nancy Davy

**The Clairemont Series**
How Far We Have Come
For Everyone, Someone
Second Chances
Meant to Be
Work in Progress
Morning Boost

**The Stephens Point Series**
The Next Lap
Right Place at the Right Time
Never Say Never

**Standalone**
Tears From My Pen
Dreaming In Color
Word Art